Bilingual Edition

Let's Draw with Shapes™

Edición Bilingüe

Let's Draw a
Butterfly with Circles

Vamos a dibujar una
mariposa usando círculos

Joanne Randolph
Ilustraciones de Emily Muschinske

Traducción al español:
María Cristina Brusca

The Rosen Publishing Group's
PowerStart Press™ & **Editorial Buenas Letras**™
New York

For Julie and Pajama Jane

Published in 2004 by The Rosen Publishing Group, Inc.
29 East 21st Street, New York, NY 10010

First Edition

Book Design: Emily Muschinske

Photo Credits: pp. 23, 24 © Royalty-Free/CORBIS.

Randolph, Joanne
Let's draw a butterfly with circles = Vamos a dibujar una mariposa usando círculos / Joanne Randolph ; illustrations by Emily Muschinske ; translated by María Cristina Brusca.
p. cm. — (Let's draw with shapes)
Includes index.
Summary: This book offers simple instructions for using circles to draw a butterfly.
  ISBN 1-4042-7500-2 (lib.)
1. Butterflies in art—Juvenile literature   2. Circle in art—Juvenile literature   3. Drawing—Technique—Juvenile literature   [1. Butterflies in art   2. Drawing—Technique 3. Spanish language materials—Bilingual]   I. Muschinske, Emily   II. Title   III. Series
  NC655.R362 2004   2003-009168
  743.6—dc21

Manufactured in the United States of America

Due to the changing nature of Internet links, PowerKids Press has developed an online list of Web sites related to the subject of this book. This site is updated regularly. Please use this link to access the list:

www.buenasletraslinks.com/ldwsh/marip/

2

Contents

Contenido

Draw a red circle to make part of a wing for your butterfly.

Dibuja un círculo rojo; así comenzarás una de las alas de tu mariposa.

5

Draw an orange circle to make part of the next wing for your butterfly.

_____

Dibuja un círculo anaranjado, para hacer la segunda ala de tu mariposa.

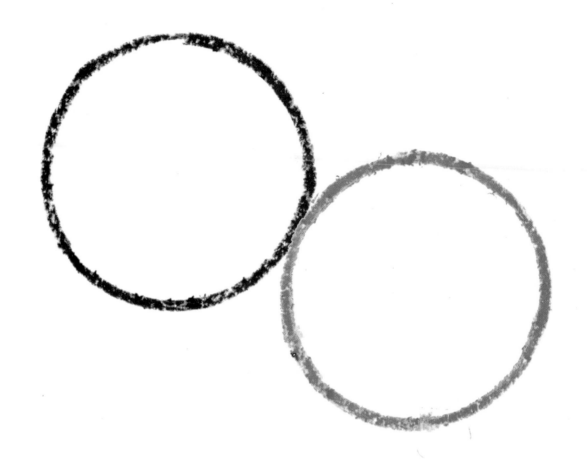

7

Add a smaller yellow circle to the right wing of your butterfly.

Agrega un círculo amarillo más pequeño en el ala derecha de tu mariposa.

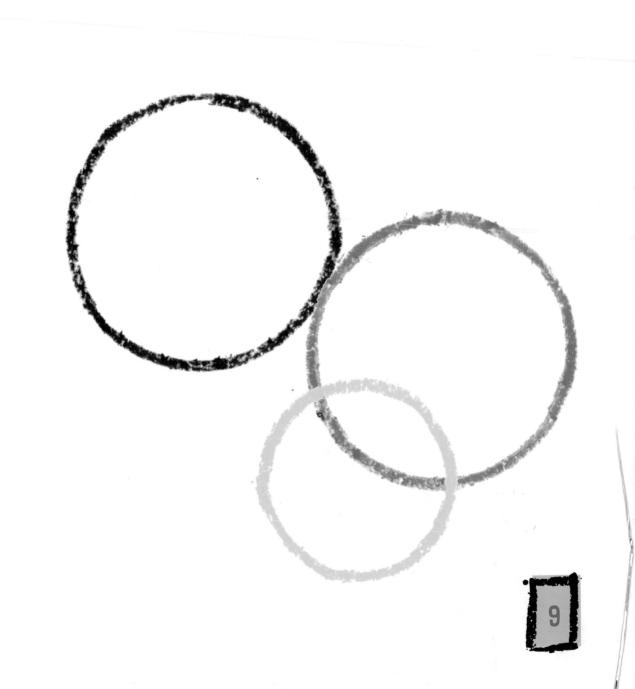

9

Add a green circle to the left wing of your butterfly.

Agrega un círculo verde en la ala izquierda de tu mariposa.

Add two small blue circles
to the wings of your
butterfly.

Agrega dos pequeños
círculos azules en las alas
de tu mariposa.

12

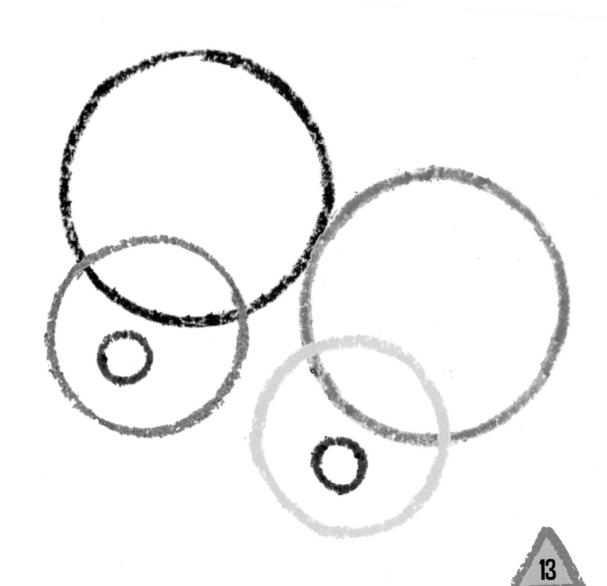

13

Add two small purple circles to the wings.

Agrega dos pequeños círculos violeta en las alas de tu mariposa.

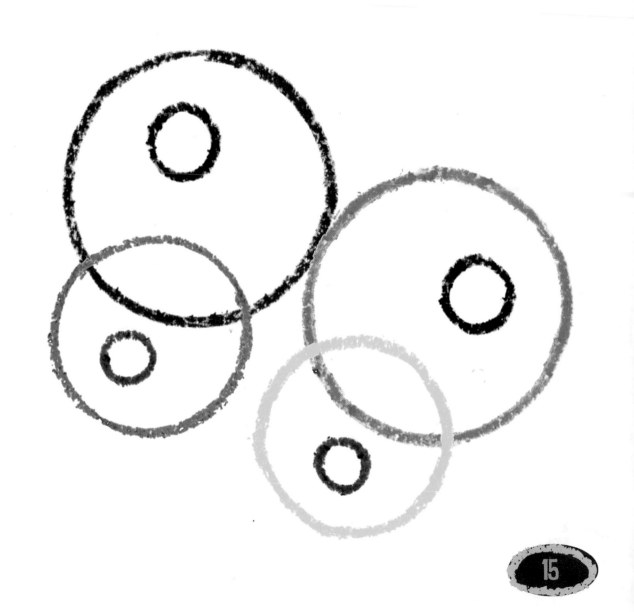

15

Draw one pink circle for the head of your butterfly.

Dibuja un círculo rosa, para hacer la cabeza de tu mariposa.

16

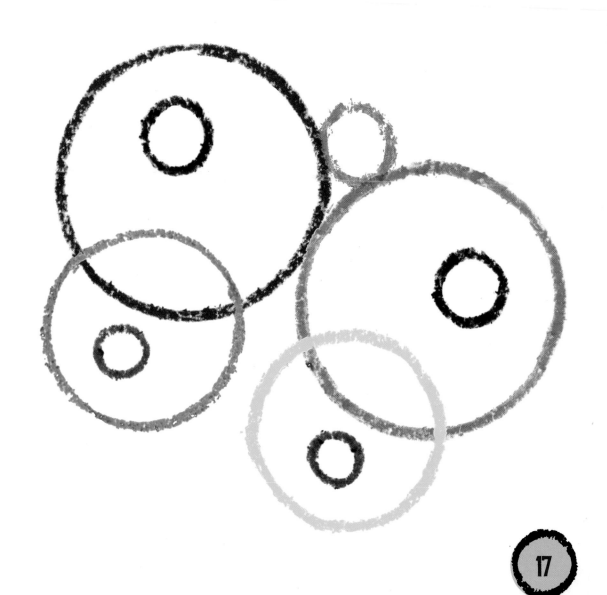

17

Draw seven black circles for the body of your butterfly.

Dibuja siete círculos
negros para hacer
el cuerpo
de tu mariposa.

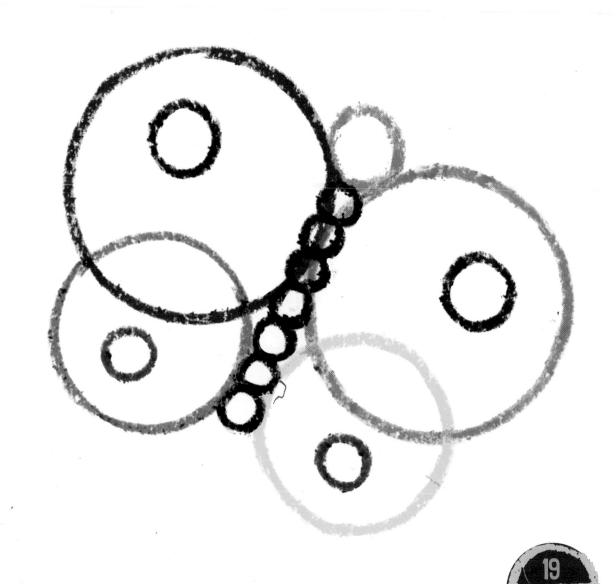

19

Color in your butterfly.

Colorea tu mariposa.

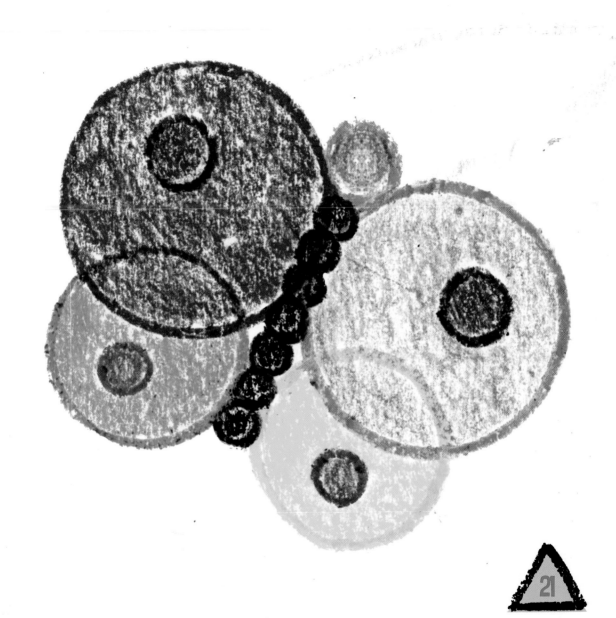

A butterfly has
many colors.

Una mariposa tiene
muchos colores.

Words to Know /
Palabras que debes saber

body /
cuerpo

butterfly /
mariposa

wing /
ala

Colors /
Colores

 red /rojo

 orange / anaranjado

yellow / amarillo

 green / verde

 blue / azul

purple / violeta

pink / rosa

black / negro